TRUST

JOHNS HOPKINS
UNIVERSITY PRESS

AARHUS UNIVERSITY PRESS

Trust

GERT TINGGAARD
SVENDSEN

TRUST

© Gert Tinggaard Svendsen
and Johns Hopkins University Press 2025
Layout and cover: Camilla Jørgensen, Trefold
Cover photograph: Poul Ib Henriksen
Publishing editor: Karina Bell Ottosen
Translated from the Danish by Heidi Flegal
Printed by Narayana Press, Denmark
Printed in Denmark 2025

ISBN 978-1-4214-4781-0 (pbk)
ISBN 978-1-4214-4782-7 (ebook)

Library of Congress Control Number: 2023942090

Special discounts are available for bulk purchases of this book. For more information, please contact Special Sales at specialsales@jh.edu.

Published in the United States by:

Johns Hopkins University Press
2715 North Charles Street
Baltimore, MD 21218
www.press.jhu.edu

Published with the generous support of the Aarhus University Research Foundation

Purchase in Denmark: ISBN 978-87-7597-523-5

Aarhus University Press
Helsingforsgade 25
8200 Aarhus N
Denmark
www.aarhusuniversitypress.dk

PEER
REVIEWED

FSC FSC® C010651

CONTENTS

KNIFE AND FORK

It is early morning. The sun is rising over the waters of the Kattegat strait, somewhere between Denmark and Sweden. The sea is calm, and dawn in this coastal setting brings a deeper meaning to the word 'tranquillity'. My family and I are camping on the island of Læsø with my younger brother, Gunnar, and his family. We do this every summer: leave the peninsula and main islands behind and go camping together on one of Denmark's several hundred smaller islands, exploring the clement shores and blue waters of this ocean-bound kingdom.

Læsø, off the north coast of the Jutland peninsula, is probably our most peaceful destination so far. It epitomises the Danish concept of *hygge*, a convivial way of spending time together on cosy, pleasant activities (often involving food and drink) and celebrating a sense of sameness. Here on the island we don't have to worry about theft, vandalism or similar disagreeable things. Nor do we need to hide our valuables, and we leave our tents and cars unlocked. Our reservation was made over the telephone, without online forms or encrypted credit-card numbers. We will pay for our stay when we leave. Theoretically, we could drive away quietly early in the morning without paying, but that would never occur to us or to any of the other campers. This is a safe, comfortable, peaceful place. When the children wake up, they run down to the beach to play or roam the campground on their own. When the babies get tired, their parents leave them to nap outside in their baby carriages.

In the words of Poul Nyrup Rasmussen, a former Danish prime minister (and no relation to other recent PMs with the same surname): You rarely see a Dane with a knife in one hand without a fork in the other. This certainly rings true on Læsø. Here, anyone can safely turn their back to a stranger holding a knife without fear of being stabbed.

Immediately after this holiday I go to a conference in South Africa, travelling directly from the peaceful island of Læsø to Durban, the second-largest city in South Africa.

As soon as I get off the plane I sense a radical difference. There are armed guards everywhere, and people hold their belongings close. On the very first day I am obliged to adjust my view of other people – to prevent the remainder of my life from becoming very chaotic and very brief. The receptionist instructs me not to open the door to my hotel room: If someone knocks, I must hide all my valuables, ask who's there, then call reception. If they can vouch for the person on the other side of the door, it's OK to open. I find myself wondering whether I will be assaulted next time I pass a stranger in the hallway.

This probably makes sense. I am visiting a society where the police force is corrupt or absent, and where lawlessness is rife in the streets – and maybe in the hotel hallways too.

On the first conference day, panic breaks out after numerous attendees are assaulted. Thugs lurking near the hotel pursue guests who venture outside carrying valuables. One sits on the victim, holding a knife to their throat, while the other searches the victim's pockets. Like a typical food-loving camper on Læsø, the muggers have a knife in one hand, but they certainly don't have a fork in the other. After a stream of complaints and insistent demands from the attendees, the organisers arrange for a bus to pick us up the next morning. We can now dash from the hotel lobby to the bus, avoiding assaults and squeezing into the bus like terrified lemmings.

I haven't done research on South Africa, and I don't know the country beyond these personal experiences, but clearly such obsessive security concerns and constant fear of others has a huge impact. It isn't easy to protect all one's valuables all the time, and such vigilance takes a lot of energy. It would be insane to behave in Durban as one would on Læsø, letting kids rove unsupervised, or strolling along the beach after dark.

Many Danes remember a news story from 1997 about a Danish woman living in New York City who left her 14-month-old daughter asleep in a baby carriage outside a café in New York City. The mother, who was sitting inside, could see her baby through the window, so in her view all was well. Then a concerned citizen called the police. They soon arrived at the scene, took the child into custody and arrested the mother. Begging to see her daughter, she was taken to the police station, strip-searched, cuffed and detained in a cell while she could hear her baby crying.

The woman was released with a warning, and mother and child were reunited. What she had failed to appreciate was that in the United States, leaving a baby outside in a carriage, unattended, is regarded as deeply irresponsible. In court the woman argued that Danes traditionally, routinely, let babies sleep outside cafés, that we do not fear kidnapping, and so on. Historically, one of just a few known examples in Denmark of someone stealing an occupied baby carriage is from 1978, when a mentally disturbed woman pushed a baby carriage along for a few blocks – and did the baby no harm.

But how should we interpret the difference between leaving a baby carriage outside a café in New York City and in Copenhagen? And what are the societal and civic consequences of similar differences between Durban and Læsø? It would take a trip from my home base in Aarhus to Washington, DC to help me identify this as my field of research.

TOP ECONOMISTS AND THEIR STUPID QUESTIONS

In the mid-1990s, I went to Washington to pursue my studies at Maryland University. My supervisor, Mancur

Olson, and his colleagues repeatedly asked me why Denmark and the other Nordic countries were performing so well, in economic and social terms.

While in Washington, I also met the Nobel laureate Douglas North. He talked about the importance of a society's institutions and norms, and like Mancur Olson, Wallace Oates, Barry Weingast and other leading economists, North was extremely interested in solving what economists called 'the Nordic puzzle': What was so special about Scandinavia? How could it be so successful? Did we have some secret resource? They simply wondered what was at the bottom of it all. I was somewhat annoyed. I had come to the US to study what was going on in America, and I really couldn't see why they found Denmark so intriguing. Also – needless to say – I felt a bit uncomfortable about not having an adequate response to their queries.

After I returned to Denmark their unrelenting questions stayed with me, and I too began to wonder, and to search for an explanation. I kept in touch with Mancur Olson, and his enthusiasm and contagious energy pushed my work in a fruitful direction. In the mid-1990s, Olson headed up a large research project for the World Bank on the concept of 'social capital', which has to do with the value of social networks. More precisely, he was tasked with finding out how social capital could be applied in developing countries.

Along with the Danish professors Martin Paldam and Peter Nannestad, I was fortunate enough to be appointed to the steering group for this project. It was an unforgettable journey with Olson at the helm. He was extremely inventive, and a great motivator. Always on the go, always eager to discuss any topic. It says volumes about Olsen's personality that after his death Maryland University dedicated a university chair in his name, to "the man who couldn't sit still".

The results of the project inspired me, and it struck me that the solution to the Nordic puzzle might be found somewhere economists rarely look. Not in the ground as raw material, nor inside people's heads as education, but rather in the relations between people. The keyword might just be *trust* – and trust was precisely the topic I was invited to speak on in Durban, the city where I had to flee violent assailants several times.

My emerging thoughts crystallised into this hypothesis: In the Nordic countries, we have a particularly large pool of trust compared to other countries, especially developing countries. In fact, our entire welfare system is founded on trust, in the sense that we are confident most others (and not just we, ourselves) will contribute to the common good. In addition, citizens must be able to trust in their public institutions, and be able to believe that tax revenues will be invested and redistributed as promised. Inversely, the authorities actually have to deliver the goods, put their money where their mouth is, and give their citizens value for money.

If you were the only honest taxpayer and you found out everybody else was shirking or moonlighting, you would feel stupid and stop paying taxes to those who were taking advantage of you. According to my hypothesis, the social trust we Danes have in other people might well be our unique raw material: the goldmine that could explain our inordinately high levels of wealth and happiness.

Reportedly, Vladimir Lenin once said that trust is good, but control is better. Is that really true? Like the other Nordic peoples, Danes are lucky to live in a highly efficient and highly trusting society. Doubtless, my personal experience of a summer's day on Læsø is not representative of how all Danes perceive their fellow human beings. Even so, it is possible to measure trust in large groups, and to establish that Danes are world leaders in trusting. Also, findings document that trust has real economic advantages.

On the following pages I will share with you the remarkable story of our trustful Danish society. This is the story I should have told Olson, Oates and Weingast all those years ago back in Washington, when they just wouldn't stop asking me stupid questions.

FROM
ICE-AGE CLAN
TO
WELFARE STATE

Social trust – meaning trust in strangers you haven't met before – is one of several types of trust. Before the last ice age, people in primitive hunter-gatherer societies, organised voluntarily into small tribes or clans (of about 50 to 150 members) to hunt and gather food. Each clan upheld a sort of mutual insurance system based on another type of trust: *individual trust* – meaning trust in someone you already know. If you were injured during a mammoth hunt, you trusted the rest of the group to care for you, not leave you to a cruel fate. Evolution favoured this type of organisation, where everyone knew and individually trusted the other clan members. Without trust, their chances of survival were slim.

In order to maintain social control and create predictable behaviour according to its shared rules, the group had to stay under a certain critical mass. Many pre-agricultural tribes had no chieftains, and if a group grew too large for all members to know each other, it would simply split in two.

This situation changed after the last ice age, around 10,000 years ago, with the advent of agriculture. New farming techniques led to a clear division of labour, more urbanisation, and huge increases in food production and populations. The social structure shifted from smaller to larger groups. Eventually social trust became a necessity, since people could no longer personally know everyone they had to deal with to survive.

This was a drastic change compared to 'the good old days' before the agricultural revolution, when people rarely left their camps, and strangers were eyed with suspicion. Surplus production created the basis for long-distance trade with towns and countries far away. A third type of trust, which develops over time in modern societies, is *institutional trust* – people's confidence in formal public bodies such as the courts, police and administration.

My story will concentrate on social trust, disregarding individual trust, for two reasons.

First, there is the problem that individual trust can affect economic growth and welfare negatively. Organisations like the mafia, terrorist groups and gangs are built on individual trust, yet what they expect is that members and associates will not betray them to the police or to other criminal groups. In practice it is extremely difficult to calculate how much a society loses in economic growth and collective welfare due to the activities of criminal organisations (known as 'the Hells Angels problem'). It is equally difficult to compare this loss to the increase in growth and collective welfare that originates in legitimate associations, civic organisations, sports clubs and the like, so essentially my first reason for not including individual trust here is a measuring problem.

Second, social trust is the most interesting element when studying the Nordic welfare model, which hinges on redistributing tax revenues among strangers, not among people with mutual individual-trust relations. This redistribution from 'the fortunate' to 'the less fortunate' can be seen as a collective insurance system. Money is transferred, say, from healthy citizens to unwell citizens, making social trust a vital part of people's everyday lives in the welfare state.

Social trust differs fundamentally from individual trust, as it is expanded to include people whom the person exhibiting trust does not know, or know of, directly. Social trust reflects a positive perception of the generalised other, and confidence that others will interact and behave decently. One's degree of social trust therefore reflects one's standard estimate of the trustworthiness of 'an unknown other'. As the American economic theorist and Nobel laureate Kenneth Arrow once put it: "Virtually every commercial transaction has within itself an element of trust". That's why social trust may also tell us something about people's ability to cooperate. The smaller a person's perceived risk of being conned, the easier it is for them to cooperate with a stranger (or institution) about whom (or which) they have incomplete information. And that is why in the following, when I talk about 'trust', I am referring to social trust.

Elinor Ostrom, an American political scientist and

Nobel laureate, writes that *voluntary cooperation* is based on self-enforcement and therefore establishes an informal institution without written rules. The opposite of this is *forced cooperation*, enforced by an authority according to formal, written rules.

Self-enforcement is based, at least in part, on social sanctions, which can be defined as some people's punishment of, or reward to, other people for performing a specific action – rather than a penalty in the legal system or a reward from the state. The Scottish economist Adam Smith gained renown as the first to see the benefits of letting people pursue their own interests in the market. Meanwhile, he also had a sound grasp of other types of interpersonal relations and their economic implications.

It was Smith, widely known as the father of liberal economics, who conceived the idea of the 'invisible hand' in the market. As early as 1766, a decade before his famous work *The Wealth of Nations* appeared, Smith observed how the level of social trust varied among countries. He concluded that the Dutch were the most trustworthy: In Holland, he wrote, people stood by their word, and there was little risk of being cheated. Not quite so today, when first place goes to a modest-sized people that lives a bit further north, on a flat peninsula and its eastern archipelago.

TOP OF THE LIST ON TRUST

As mentioned, social trust can be measured, as the percentage of the population answering "yes" when asked whether they believe most other people can be trusted. This question is employed within the ongoing World Values Surveys, providing us with internationally comparable data across various countries worldwide.

The Nordic countries exhibit remarkable prominence in terms of social trust, positioning them as global leaders in this domain. While the Nordics can certainly acquire valuable insights from other nations, their exceptional levels of trust render them distinct. Noteworthy among these countries is Denmark with a trust rate of 77 %. The Danes are world champions in trust. Close behind Denmark is Norway with 75 %. Finland, with a trust rate of 72 %, and Sweden, with a trust rate of 67 %, also hold prominent positions. Iceland completes this impressive roster, recording a trust rate of 66 %.

Subsequent to the Nordic countries, the Netherlands emerges with a trust rate of 62 %. Additionally, other notable examples with relatively high levels of trust include Germany (46 %), the United Kingdom (41 %), and Spain (41 %). Comparatively, the United States exhibits a lower level of trust at 40 %, approximately half the level of Denmark. The average social trust level across all countries stands at 28 %. Both Italy (28 %) and France (28 %) align with this global average.

Russia demonstrates a trust rate of 24 %, while Turkey exhibits 14 %. Romania follows with a score of 12 %, succeeded by Mexico at 10 %. Greece falls below the 10% threshold, recording 8 % trust. The Philippines (5 %), Indonesia (5 %), Colombia (5 %), Nicaragua (4 %),

Albania (3 %), and finally Zimbabwe with the lowest trust level worldwide (2 %).

When asked whether they trust four crucial public institutions in their country (the government, legal system, police and bureaucrats), Denmark once again scores highest at 84%, whereas Ecuador scores lowest at 10%. In other words, 9 out of 10 Ecuadorians do not trust their institutions – a thought-provoking result. And if a country's citizens do not trust its institutions, it's harder to make them respect the law and pay taxes. People know the laws work not for them but for the power elite, and they are convinced taxes will end up in the wrong pockets. In Ecuador only fools pay taxes, because everyone knows their neighbours don't.

So Denmark and her four Nordic neighbours top the list on social trust. These high scores mean the risk of being cheated by freeriders is seen as small, which promotes informal cooperation.

We Danes are lucky to still be living in a very trusting society. I say "still" because it's no law of nature that our society should work this way. It only does so because we remain trustworthy to each other.

THE BUMBLEBEE

For many years Denmark's economic and social success seemed to defy the laws of economics. That was the gist of those relentless questions from the economists in Washington. Denmark was a lot like the bumblebee, which seemed to defy the laws of gravity: From what entomologists knew of the bumblebee's weight, wings and patterns of motion, they concluded this insect was technically unable to fly. It simply lacked sufficient lift. Fortunately the bumblebee, unaware of this, flew just fine – even before the entomologists unravelled its secrets.

Post-war Denmark has been, and remains, one of the most affluent countries in the world, despite its dearth of natural resources, its moderate education levels, a system based on heavy taxes, and massive income-transfer programmes that don't exactly prod citizens to work hard. When explained, the system sounds like it encourages Danes to siphon off rather than pitch in. For many, it would make more sense to freeride, partaking from the long list of welfare benefits without paying taxes. In a swinging 1940s evergreen, the Danish pianist Leo Mathisen and his big band satirically advised listeners to "Take it easy boy, boy. Let the others do the hard work for you." That's how you might expect most Danes to think, and act.

Actually, without risking an awful lot, many Danes could receive benefits, moonlight on the side, and let others pay taxes. In a microperspective: Why not gain a tiny advantage by throwing your litter in the street, then let others clean it up? Just the other day I was cycling to work. A bus stopped, and a beautiful blonde got off. She walked directly out onto the bicycle path, crossing it in front of me without looking. Law-abiding cyclist that I am, I was prepared for this sort of thing and stopped short of hitting her. She was chewing gum, and to my surprise she spat it out, right there on the sidewalk, about half a metre from a litter bin. She saved herself the trouble of taking an extra step to reach the bin ... but others would have to step in her gum, or pick it up after her.

Now let me ask: Did you notice the phrase "to my surprise"? Probably not. Most likely, you also found her behaviour odd. You didn't stop and think: "Hang on: That's no surprise. Why would she take an extra step? She won't have to step in that gob of gum herself." The point is, her conduct is anomalous, hence our surprise. Luckily, leaving the hard work to others has not become widespread in Denmark. Yet. Most Danes are still 'every-day heroes'. Decent folk who go to work every day, each doing their bit to keep the wheels turning, cooperating with others, paying taxes and taking that extra step to put their gum in the litter bin.

For half a century, Denmark's economy has been flying high – confounding economists. Perhaps now we have the answer: trust. The invisible jet fuel that gives Denmark its extra lift.

Economists have calculated that physical capital (the means of production and the infrastructure) explains one fourth of Denmark's wealth, and that human capital (the population's level of education and innovation) explains half, but until recently they haven't been able to explain the remaining fourth. Trust, despite its many advantages, was long left out of the economic equation.

When everything doesn't have to be set down in writing, citizens and societies can save lots of time and effort. If other people are generally trustworthy and decent, citizens and companies can avoid a range of expenses, like fees to lawyers or enforcers hired to collect money from an employer or buyer who suddenly refuses to pay. In Denmark we rarely see armed guards in front of supermarkets or banks, a common sight in other, less trusting countries, where some might say: Control is best exercised with a gun in your hand.

Danes save large sums of money every year because we file relatively fewer lawsuits than other nationalities. We spend less on litigation, and on burglar alarms and security. We can use our money better than low-trust countries because we don't feel obliged to spend it on control. Such savings give us a competitive edge compared to countries with extensive fraud and crime, where people must constantly spend time and money on protection and remedial action.

The trust level among Danes is a matchless resource for businesses and citizens alike. Danish businesses are known, among other things, for their ability and willingness to cooperate without comprehensive, expensive, formal contracts. They often make binding oral agreements, giving the added bonus of avoiding misunderstandings, since the transaction is based on direct communication.

One of my favourite examples is from a candid interview with the managing director of a machine factory in Jutland:

We don't do signed contracts with our customers. Sure, sometimes we get burned. Some customers just vanish, and we're stuck with the extra stock. [...] Then again, sometimes we benefit from overproducing because it allows us to take in quick orders … like when a customer forgot to order. That sort of thing … One time, we negotiated with a turbine manufacturer, where you had to sign this and that, and hire a lawyer and … I guess we just don't have the time or the inclination for that, you know? That sort of partnership, nah … If you can talk your way to, well, to a mutual understanding and stick to your word, then that's it, see? And it keeps us from drowning in paperwork, which only makes for more expenses and more hassle, and we'd have to bring in lawyers to actually get around to making something. I mean, we're not some kind of paper mill; we're a factory that makes machines. So no, we don't waste our energy on that.

It seems a convincing case: A man saves money by running his factory on trust rather than bothering with loads of paperwork. If he did insist on rules and contracts he would need professional assistance, so if trust were low and contracts necessary, the factory would also have several legal sticklers on the payroll and be less competitive.

You may have heard the joke about the man who goes to see a lawyer? The man walks into the lawyer's office and says, "Hello. How much does it cost to hire a lawyer?" "Well," the lawyer replies, "the fee is 500 dollars per question." "Isn't that a bit expensive?" the man says. "No, I don't think so," says the lawyer. "Now what was your third question?"

If trust disappears, a society runs less smoothly and things get more complicated. Legal fees rise, as do complaints and lawsuits springing from mistrust. In such a society people can't even count on the legal system to guarantee justice, because their opponent may have bribed the judge.

As for universities, rather than the smartest applicants they may accept those who have bribed their way to good exam results – which, from a societal perspective, is academic resource mismanagement.

Perhaps trust can also alleviate shocks to a country's economy? Countries with higher social-trust levels actually do seem better equipped to handle a financial crisis. A lacking buffer of social trust might explain why people flocked to the banks to withdraw their money during the global financial panic of 2008. The average world citizen has far less trust in others than the average Nordic citizen. This is conducive to fear. Fear that everyone else will rush to the bank to take out their money. That makes it important to get there before all the cash is gone. Such reactions may seem irrational when households, businesses and most banks are fairly sound, and obviously from a financial perspective this response pattern is undesirable.

The problem is, if you have reason to fear the worst from others – in this case, a financial knee-jerk reaction – the only sane thing to do is switch to autopilot, put on your darkest sunglasses and put your own interests first. In many places the financial crisis kick-started a negative spiral. The population (financial advisors included) got jittery, and the general trust in banks, politicians, businesses and customers plummeted.

When such mistrust rises, people reduce consumption and investments drastically in an attempt to protect their assets, but this merely puts more pressure on businesses and increases fear of unemployment. Low levels of trust can make financial advisors restrict loan options, which in turn paralyses credit markets and exacerbates the crisis.

Social trust is important because it may help ease a financial crisis to a more acceptable level. A country in dire economic straits can draw on social trust, whereas people in low-trust societies are more reluctant to trust advice from the financial sector. If social trust is in short supply, an economic shock will more likely turn citizens into Robinson Crusoes who forget all about cooperation and social responsibility. This just makes the situation worse. The problem behind an escalating financial crisis is not only the challenges to banks and stock markets, but also the relatively low trust levels in affected populations.

High trust levels in the Nordic region indicate that citizens there are less likely to panic in a crisis and rush to the bank to withdraw their money, for instance. Being less generally distrustful, they have more faith that others will not panic either. In other words, luckily for Denmark, most Danes lean towards the title of Leo Mathisen's old swing hit – *Take it easy boy, boy* – while not heeding its witty advice to let others do the hard work.

THE ORIGINS OF TRUST

Trust itself does not appear out of the blue. Neither does the idea of trust as an important piece in the economic development puzzle. Economic growth theory was founded after World War II. Since then, the social sciences have gradually accepted how strongly economic growth is affected by informal institutions – one of which is trust.

Economic thinking in the post-war era falls into three main stages. During the first stage, from around 1945 to 1980, the state was seen as 'good'. Public institutions were perceived as competent, efficient bodies that spent taxpayer money well on delivering various so-called collective goods (roads, hospitals, courts and so forth). The early economists therefore wrote of extensive state intervention in the market economy and production processes as positive for economic growth. At the same time, the deep recession in the interwar years had given rise to widespread pessimism about the market's ability to foster growth.

Today, the entire EU system is based on this line of thought, which has its legislative roots in the European Commission. The chief architect behind today's European Union, the French bureaucrat Jean Monnet, proposed attributing the right to initiate legislation to the Commission (that is, the bureaucracy) rather than to a parliamentary body. Enlightened and benevolent bureaucrats would ensure a peaceful and prosperous Europe, the reasoning went. Since then, the European Parliament has gradually gained power, but the Commission remains the central authority and still decides on legislation.

The second stage, from around 1980 to 1990, was largely a reaction against the left-wing intellectuals of the 1970s. In this stage, the state came to be seen as 'evil'. Public institutions 'shackled the market' by favouring narrow interests, politicians and bureaucrats. The view was that public institutions based their actions on narrow self-interest, spending the money on themselves instead of advancing collective goods that would benefit society at large. Many argued that politicians and bureaucrats thought only of themselves, forgetting to serve their community and country. And when the state becomes too big and money ends up in the wrong pockets, economic growth slows down.

The trends in this 'neoclassical counterrevolution' were privatisation and a minimal state apparatus. Notably conservative governments in the US (under Ronald Reagan) and the UK (under Margaret Thatcher) invoked the market forces as a solution. As incoming president Ronald Reagan insisted in 1981, in his inaugural address: "government is not the solution to our problem; government *is* the problem." Successful examples of this strategy are New Zealand and the four Asian tigers (South Korea, Taiwan, Hong Kong and Singapore), so we cannot say the philosophy is wrong. It was simply unable to explain certain developments – including the economic success of the Nordic countries.

During the third stage of modern economic growth theory, since about 1990, public institutions have come sharply into focus. Many authors have attempted to compare the *quality* of these institutions by examining the state's ability to provide collective goods. The question is not whether the public sector is good or evil per se, but rather whether public institutions in various countries have been able to introduce and implement 'good' policies that increase economic growth, regardless of potential special interests and corruption.

In his inaugural address in January 2009, another incoming US president, Barack Obama, clearly articulated this new perspective: "The question we ask today is not whether our government is too big or too small, but whether it works." Mancur Olson, my inspirational mentor, also concluded that the main reason why some countries are rich and others poor lies in qualitative differences in their public institutions and resulting economic policies.

The latest trend in growth theory is a shift from formal institutions to informal institutions – the latter being values, norms and human relations. As social trust may well be 'the missing link' in economic growth theory, we can fairly assume that social trust might also be a new production factor, alongside the two conventional production factors: human and physical capital. That makes it relevant to explore the topic of institutional competitiveness based on informal rules.

I recently lost my wallet at a Danish airport. It was dropped, not stolen. The wallet and its contents (cash to the tune of 400 euros, my passport, visa, cards and more) were handed in to the airport staff. They paged me over the PA system. I was soon happily reunited with my wallet – by which time the anonymous finder was long gone. This auspicious incident reminded me of the ancient legend of King Frode Fredegod, who ostensibly brought peace and prosperity to Denmark. He left his golden ring at the roadside, trusting that no one would steal it. Years later when he returned, the ring was still there, waiting for its rightful owner.

The king's story is merely a legend, of course, and my experience at the airport is just an uplifting anecdote. Still, such incidents are more than strokes of good luck. In several international experiments, wallets with valuable contents have been 'lost' on main streets around the world. In Scandinavia, most were handed in intact, with return rates highest in Denmark and Norway. This demonstrates that Scandinavians really can be trusted, and that they trust the authorities. If the police pocketed the money and threw away the wallets, people would see no point in handing them in.

Another example of the exceptional trust in Scandinavia is found in Norway, whose vast, untamed mountain ranges are dotted with lodges and cabins run by the Norwegian Trekking Association, DNT. Thanks to its trust-based system, all DNT members can use these often unstaffed cabins as they hike, bike or ski through the wilderness. Each self-service cabin has a well-stocked larder, effectively making a nationwide network of shelters and provisions accessible to all key-carrying members of DNT – currently some 300,000 people. When leaving, visitors fill out a slip with their name, food and drink consumption, and account number for payment. This easy, practical system would be unthinkable almost anywhere else in the world.

Then there are the vegetables, fruit and other products offered for sale in humble stalls along Danish roadsides. Passers-by can browse the shelves, take what they want and drop payment into a jar or cigar box. This unstaffed sales system is extremely efficient – when it works. In Denmark, it usually does. Anyone could steal the produce or the money, and a typical Brazilian or South African would think the farmers and gardeners who use this system almost absurdly naive.

Trust even comes into play when people ask for directions, and Danes give (and expect to get) straight answers, not deliberately wrong answers as in some countries. Also, anonymous passers-by often hang up lost personal items on Danish hedgerows or fences: The owner may cycle past tomorrow and spot their missing mitten or scarf.

Individuals are probably rewarded for such trusting

behaviour with greater happiness: It feels good! Showing and receiving trust is pleasant, just as being accused of cheating or lying is unpleasant. Also, cooperating creates a diminutive high: Collaborating and volunteering causes the brain to release the reward hormone oxytocin, which brings a sense of well-being. Mind you, these emerging neurobiological findings are still hotly debated, but besides leading in trust, Danes are also world leaders in happiness. That is a different story, however, best saved for another spell of reflection.

We still don't know enough about how social trust is generated. In this young research field we've probably just scratched the surface, but trust is a significant topic. If social trust really is the key to the Nordic puzzle, we must uncover the origins of trust as a resource. That's why the next step is to collect extensive historical data, so we can compare social trust in Scandinavia and other countries. New insights can help optimise the quantity of trust in a given society, prevent the erosion of social trust and reinforce trust over time.

An important part of this involves uncovering the origins of Denmark's gold: its outstanding reserve of social trust. The resource which, in all likelihood, makes the society and economy in Denmark run more smoothly than in many other countries, and makes it a better place to live.

There are many theories about the origins of trust. Let's look at three of the most important explanations: the welfare state, cultural heritage and political stability.

The big question in the literature is still the causal flow of these factors, much like the chicken and the egg: Do the institutions of the welfare state generate social trust, or does a pre-existing reserve of social trust enable the survival of the welfare state? Or is there a reciprocal effect between trust and the welfare state?

CORRUPTION AND THE WELFARE STATE

Initially, one explanation might be that a non-corrupt welfare state reliably providing common goods through education, redistribution and equality will engender trust. It is plausible that equality reduces the amount of social conflict and the risk of being mugged in the street – unlike in, say, South Africa, where impoverished muggers have everything to gain and virtually nothing to lose.

In welfare states, effective public institutions that limit corruption and wrongdoing and promote education, in turn giving citizens a better understanding of their society, presumably also create a framework that fosters trust.

Consider a commercial lawsuit about a purchase contract. Here it is important that justice be served by the 'right' party winning the dispute. If a swindler can bribe the judge and win a case, the picture of future rulings becomes blurred, and it becomes harder for commercial partners to rely on social trust. They will be forced to take precautions against fraud – even if they have a signed contract. The Swedish political scientist Bo

Rothstein advocates the 'institutions matter' approach, arguing that the quality of welfare institutions is the main explanation for a given society's social-trust level. His main conclusion is that the less corrupt (and the more impartial) public institutions are, the higher the level of social trust will be. Why 'trust most people' if you know people will generally bribe, cheat, threaten or murder others without the police intervening?

South American and African countries with low trust levels typically have widespread corruption and ineffective public authorities, whereas corruption is rare in the Nordic region. International studies and Transparency International often list the Nordic countries as the least corrupt in the world. This is a great advantage when foreign companies are considering a market entry. Besides potential benefits from higher trust, low corruption makes many foreign companies want to invest and operate in Scandinavia. Predictability, stability and the absence of extra costs arising from corruption mean that the companies receiving orders and permits are the *best* companies, not those that have bribed bureaucrats. This promotes healthy competition and efficient business processes, contributing to economic growth.

A colleague once told me about a holiday in Jordan, where he was visiting friends. He was driving slowly along the crowded streets of Amman when an old man threw himself in front of the car. My colleague stepped on the brakes and did not hit the man, who nevertheless stayed on the ground, writhing in pain and wailing loudly, as though he had been hit. The police arrived, arrested my colleague and threw him in jail. After three days in a filthy Jordanian prison he appeared before a judge and was sentenced to pay damages to compensate the old man. After my colleague had paid up and been released, his friends explained that the old man obviously made a living throwing himself in front of tourist-driven cars, then split his compensation with the police and the judge.

In societies that unjustly favour certain people, citizens gradually lose trust in public officials and institutions, as seen over recent years in several North African countries, where popular protest movements have put pressure on the power elite. In other low-trust countries like Zimbabwe, Afghanistan, Somalia and Iraq, constant infighting among clans based on family ties, religion or political views is having a devastating impact.

In Iraq the roots of distrust, corruption and violence clearly run deep. The Iraqi expatriate Fuad Suleiman has described life in Iraq before the American invasion as follows:

> Corruption prevailed in Government ranks. Corruption is not so rare in developing governments, and even not so rare in some leading developed societies, but it was pervasive in tightly controlled Iraq. I was struck by the fraying social bonds in the society at large. Iraqis had been raised to inform on their neighbors, to distrust each other, to suspect anyone

who offered a helping hand, and to obey anyone in authority.

Financially, corrupt countries suffer a double whammy: Besides reducing trust and growth, corruption puts money in the wrong hands. Meanwhile, journalists and others in the public arena often hesitate to speak out on corruption because they fear reprisals, or even death.

The best advice, as a first step, for any country that wants to maintain and increase its reserve of social trust, is to preserve and improve the quality of its institutions by effectively fighting corruption.

The low corruption level in Denmark is good for businesses, and for tourism, mutual trust among Danes, and the trust foreign investors and individuals have in Denmark. It also promotes efficiency, with a merit-based system where people can climb the ladder if they want to, provided they have the right skills. You don't have to know the right people to get ahead. As a result, employees are well-suited for their jobs, and combined with high trust this gives Denmark a crucial competitive edge.

In many ways, Denmark is a model of how less corruption and better institutions can promote trust and economic growth. The prevalent corruption in Southern and Eastern Europe shows the exact opposite, and that is where the EU can apply the Danish model. A corruption ranking of EU countries yields almost the same pattern as a trust ranking. Corruption is lowest, and trust highest, in the Nordics. The further south we look, the more corruption and the less trust we see.

Assuming that trust is somehow inversely proportionate to corruption, then based on the Danish model it is plausible that less corruption and better institutions will boost trust and economic growth. Hence, the political recommendation to the EU is to effectively combat corruption – especially in Southern Europe and the newer Eastern European member states – to reap the double benefits of more trust and less corruption.

Several reports show that Denmark leads the EU in reforms that foster economic growth and promote employment. Not surprisingly, European economists are exploring how the Danish welfare model might be copied. Sweden and Austria also rank high on such reforms, while Italy and Poland rank low. Clearly it is hard to break the negative spiral, even for countries in Southern and Eastern Europe that are actively battling corruption.

To sum up: Corruption increases expenses and makes investments unsafe, and the best businesses miss out on contracts. The result: unequal competition. When the businesses with the best price or the best quality don't get the orders, overall efficiency suffers. This seriously obstructs economic and social growth. The huge variations in income and reform-readiness are a problem for EU's objectives to become the world's most competitive economy, and to increase social cohesion.

Interestingly, in other international studies Danes also score highest on two other dimensions: 'courtesy and kindness towards others' and 'openness to new ideas and opportunities'. That is another reason why the EU as a whole, in its efforts to reach its objectives, could benefit from Scandinavia's experience with universal welfare models in the light of economic efficiency and social cohesion.

Effective, non-corrupt institutions are important preconditions for trust-generating societies. Findings indicate that such institutions are difficult to export to, say, developing countries with low trust. That's the bad news. But there may be good news, too: Governments and public bodies can take the lead by walking the talk. They can highlight good examples from their own country's history, fight corruption, and generally try to help citizens behave decently, promoting trust creation from the bottom up.

All in all, institutional quality and equal access to public services indicate a way forward, in an approach where institutions matter, and where the causal flow mainly runs from institutional design to social trust. Yet as I suggested earlier, this causality may also run the other way.

TRUST IN A CULTURAL CONTEXT

A second explanation is that the creation of trust is culturally determined and occurs slowly over time. If so, Denmark has been accumulating a large reserve of social trust over many years. Like a great body of water, this pool of trust supports the raft of the comprehensive welfare system we have built on it, keeping the raft afloat. Due to the high level of pre-existing trust, the vast majority of Danes have been contributors, not freeriders.

The American political scientist Eric Uslaner is an excellent representative of the authors who (unlike Rothstein and others) argue that the causal flow runs from culturally determined trust norms to the formation of welfare states, along with associations and clubs. He refers to studies that show how children learn social trust early in life from parents and schools, and how trust levels remain stable throughout their lives. Uslaner claims that trust passed on from parents can be traced back to grandparents and earlier ancestors, so immigrants may well carry social trust with them to their new country. Intriguingly, the grandparents of the most trustful people in the US were originally from the Nordic countries. Americans with Danish, Norwegian, Swedish or Finnish ancestors have roughly 10% more social trust than the American population on average, as do their descendants.

Given that immigrants' trust scores were not affected by their move to the US, the numbers indicate that trust levels in the Nordic countries have been stable and high for generations. Now suppose social trust actually has deep historical roots and is transferred early in life to children by parents and schools; and that such acquired trust norms remain largely unchanged throughout life; and that trust is exceptionally stable over time. If this is true, then Danish immigrants to the US brought their high trust level with them and retained it for generations rather than dropping to the average US level.

Pursuing this line of thought, Danish schools not only teach their pupils to read and write, they also pass on a set of norms – so Denmark's municipal school system, secondary schools, folk high schools, continuation schools, night schools and other educational settings impart social training to pupils and students. This is an important element in conveying trust, and my best unscientific guess would be that schools probably merit more credit here than they get.

Culturally determined trust in a society may also be based on religion. The Protestant ethic, for instance, is often said to emphasise thrift, integrity and hard work, as "in the sweat of thy face shalt thou eat bread" (Genesis 3:19). A noteworthy correlation shows that Northern European countries, which are largely Protestant, have 28% more social trust than the largely Catholic countries of Southern Europe.

Immigration to Denmark from low-trust countries is another interesting phenomenon. What happens, trust-wise, when people move from a low-trust to a high-trust country? Several studies indicate that they gradually adapt to the trust level in their new home, so living in Denmark raises the trust level of most immigrants here.

Over two decades (1980–2001) the number of immigrants from non-Western countries to Denmark rose from 152,958 to 415,331 or from 3.0% to 7.7% of the total population. Family reunification created the largest category of newcomers until the early 1980s, when asylum-seekers also became a major category. Today, the country's six largest ethnic groups of non-Danish ancestry are from Turkey, former Yugoslavia, Iraq, the Palestinian territories, Pakistan and Somalia. Unemployment among immigrants from non-Western countries – even those who have lived in Denmark for many years – is three times higher than among ethnic Danes. Integration through the labour market has generally failed, due to the immigrants' inferior education and qualifications, discrimination, and a lack of incentives caused by the welfare benefits they receive.

These developments have resulted in so-called parallel societies, where immigrants of certain ethnicities live in particular neighbourhoods, speak their own languages, and practice a sort of elective self-segregation, isolated from Danish society at large. The Nordic welfare model takes away much of the incentive immigrants have to find jobs. Even so, all major political parties in the Nordic countries insist on preserving their respective welfare states in their present form. By way of example, a recent Danish coalition government made up of right-of-centre, liberal parties came to power based on a convincing promise that it would *not* seek to reduce the scope of the welfare state.

This situation seems deadlocked. On the one hand, voters want to preserve the welfare state in its current form. Major reforms to reduce social benefits or services are out of the question. On the other hand, the Danish welfare state does not seem fully functional in dealing with the economic pressures of immigration, or with the forming of parallel societies with higher-than-average rates of unemployment, social problems and crime.

Short-term political reactions have been drastic, with the Nordic countries building legal walls to protect their wealth and institutions against an invasion of poor people from non-Western countries. Complex immigration rules are now in place to ensure the welfare state's survival in its present form.

This account may seem to imply that immigrants in Denmark are 'alienated', trusting only their own ethnic groups and not generally trusting native Danes or other ethnic groups. However, the findings of professor Peter Nannestad indicate that trust prevails in the way immigrants perceive ethnic Danes. For example, Turks living in Denmark trust ethnic Danes more than they trust others of Turkish descent.

Evidently, non-Western immigrants adapt somewhat to a higher trust level in their new country. Also, although parents retain the lower trust level from their home country to some extent, their children – descendants in the first and second generations – adapt more to the Danish trust level.

These studies indicate that despite the emergence of parallel societies in Denmark, immigrants' higher trust levels (compared to trust levels in their home countries), combined with their relatively high trust in Danes (compared to trust in their own ethnic groups) may create a positive and hitherto unexploited potential for better integration and co-operation in the future.

Living in Denmark seems to affect people's trust positively. Why? Possibly, since most Danes carry and convey high social trust, immigrants rarely feel cheated in their daily lives, by other people or by the authorities.

Interacting with fair teachers in the Danish school system is especially crucial in breaking inherited distrust, which some young immigrants carry with them. When they find that Danish teachers treat everyone as equal, regardless of ethnic background, this contributes to a general perception that Danish institutions are fair and impartial – a key factor in promoting adaptation to the high Danish trust level.

According to the American political scientist Robert Putnam, trust can be created through the personal contacts nurtured in clubs, associations, volunteer groups and the like, and in small communities. This individual trust (explained earlier) spreads out and permeates the wider community as social trust, which applies to 'most other people'. Putnam believes the reason for the steep decline in social trust in the US is that post-war generations spent, and spend, their time in front of television screens instead of meeting face to face and creating and maintaining social trust in personal, interactive contexts. Putnam laconically sums up this phenomenon as 'the privatisation of leisure time'.

Denmark has a deep-seated, pervasive culture of organising into private societies, co-ops and associations, large and small, which also helps explain the country's high trust level. As an old tongue-in-cheek description of this Danish penchant goes: "When two Danes meet, they shake hands. When three Danes meet, they set up an association." Or in the words of Palle Lauring, a notable Danish twentieth-century historian: "Denmark is a co-op."

The Danish co-operative movement, which gained a phenomenal following in the mid-1860s and still lives on, is doubtless another factor behind the country's high social trust. Co-ops grew from the grass roots, nurtured by local enthusiasts in rural areas, many of whom were members of several co-ops simultaneously. This created open, durable networks that were highly inclusive generators of trust. The co-op model was adopted by groups in Denmark and elsewhere who set up dairies, slaughterhouses, grain and feed stores, communal freezer houses, waterworks, local power stations, mills, and a host of other shared facilities and equipment.

The co-op movement was inspired by entirely new modes of financial organisation. In the early 1800s, Denmark was a distinctly unequal society in economic and financial terms. Poverty was endemic among the steadily growing number of smallhold farmers. The Danish war effort against England during the Napoleonic Wars would cost the country dearly, which resulted in high inflation and in turn cut deep social rifts in the Danish population. In 1807, the country was humiliated when the English navy bombarded Copenhagen and captured the Danish fleet. Then in 1813, after entering an alliance with France, the country was defeated for good. To add insult to injury, Denmark also went bankrupt that year and then lost Norway in 1814.

Widespread poverty and the absence of social-security measures forced peasants to invent their own insurance system. The result was a series of financial associations with voluntary membership. The first private credit institution was established in 1810, followed by associations for mutual fire and livestock insurance, illness benefits, rural savings and loan associations, and more. The members and elected representatives of each association would meet and set out their principles and by-laws.

The co-operative mindset also came to dominate Denmark's cultural life, spreading to intellectual and political movements and pioneering efforts to educate the population at large (in 'folk high schools' and 'free schools'), youth and community-hall movements, and political parties. Such voluntary organisations make it harder for people to cheat one other, knowing they will see the others at the association's next weekly meeting. This observation has been confirmed by several other trust researchers, who have highlighted face-to-face contact as an important factor in creating trust.

Generally, the cultural explanation of trust creation claims that we stand on the shoulders of our ancestors. Particularly if we want to preserve 'the Danish welfare bumblebee' and its ability to fly, we should reflect on and understand how such a collective insurance scheme was able to become airborne in Denmark, of all countries, rather than in, say, Burkina Faso, Iraq, Brazil or the US.

THANK THE ROWDY VIKINGS

A third explanation of the high trust scores may be the long-standing relative political stability in Denmark, and in Scandinavia at large.

Recent research indicates that if people live for long periods with sound, stable, transparent democratic institutions (courts, fair elections and so on) and, not least, with a low level of corruption, then trust can grow from the bottom up.

Denmark has been a fairly peaceful place since the Viking Age, about a thousand years ago, enabling its people to slowly climb 'the ladder of trust'. In contrast, Germany and France, not to mention former Communist countries such as Poland, Hungary and Romania, have been through troubles that likely pushed them off the trust ladder several times, landing them back at the bottom rung. Fortunately for Denmark, in spite of various wars and battles, the country's location on Europe's fringes spared Danes the utter devastation of the great wars and bloody revolutions.

The reason Denmark has so much social trust and a country like Poland has so little may be that Poland's original social-trust reserve was destroyed by the Communist regime in just a few years, starting with the coup in 1948. Apparently, in certain situations social trust can be destroyed incredibly fast, whereas generating social trust probably takes generations. Poland, it would seem, has not yet generated a new, large reserve of social trust after the collapse of the USSR in 1989. Most studies estimate the loss of trust due to the Communist dictatorship at about 10%. This loss has not yet been recouped, even during the twenty-some years since the country was reunited with the West and enabled to improve its institutions.

Russia's history superbly illustrates the anatomy of distrust, as seen in these two examples. The first is from a reported conversation between the Russian writer Maxim Gorky and an agent from the tsarist police, around 1890. The agent, who (rightly) suspects Gorky of anti-tsarist activity, is attempting to intimidate the writer with this description of the big 'web':

> An invisible thread, like a spider's web, emanates from the heart of His Imperial Majesty, the Tsar and Emperor Alexander III and so forth, it passes through their lordships the Ministers, then through His High Excellency the Governor, and down through all grades till it reaches me and even the lowest rank and file soldier. All is bound and knit by that thread, and it is by its invisible strength that the Tsar's empire is upheld forever and in eternity.

In the second example from 1987, the writer and dissident Vladimir Bukovsky gives an unforgettable description of the mental climate in post-war USSR:

> [Soviet man] is astonished by the ease of Westerners – not only in terms of clothes and behaviour, but also their movements and gestures. With these indefinable qualities a foreigner is always recognized in the streets of Moscow. Where do they get it from? And suddenly you realize: Eureka! It's because of FREEDOM. These bloody foreigners have never felt that something invisible was standing behind them, or the state's penetrating eyes following their every movement. They can't even imagine that someone would approach them in a menacing way and ask: 'What are you doing here?'

A well-known anecdote from 1940 tells of how King Christian X (grandfather of Denmark's reigning monarch, Queen Margrethe II) would ride through Copenhagen each morning on horseback. A foreigner in the newly occupied capital stopped a messenger boy in the street and asked, "Say, who is that tall officer riding over there?" "That's no officer," said the lad, "that's the King." "But who watches out for him?" the man exclaimed. The response came promptly: "We all do." Indeed, the last regicide in Denmark is the still-unsolved assassination of King Erik Klipping – in a barn on a dark Jutland moor in 1286.

So the stability of Denmark's institutions over time

may help explain the development of its trust and its welfare institutions, such as the famous 'Danish labour-market model' with its high degree of built-in 'flexicurity'. The country has a publicly funded financial safety net that supports unemployed wage earners. Essentially, this is an expensive, collective insurance system. In the flexicurity model, the 'social partners' – employers and employees, through their respective organisations – negotiate labour-market conditions, ideally without political interference. Ultimately they reach collective agreements that both sides will adhere to for the next three years.

Based on the country's generous public welfare benefits, the social partners have been able to reach collective agreements that make it relatively easy for employers to dismiss employees who are no longer needed. But to convince employees to give up certain privileges, they must be offered something in return. This trade-off lies at the very core of the flexicurity strategy. Imagine you are a tight-rope walker getting ready to cross a deep canyon. You agree to cross, but only if there is a safety net underneath, to catch you if you fall. This is the Danish wage-earner in a nutshell.

For society as a whole, it is important that individual employees are willing to try something new, and that individual companies are willing to test new ideas. Many Danish companies dare to launch innovative projects because those that fail can be terminated; a complicated process if laws or agreements make employee dismissals all but impossible.

It is reasonable to suggest that the Danish labour-market model has grown out of the pool of trust between employers and employees, which has been slowly accumulating since the late 1800s. This model is admired throughout Europe for its ability to create growth and stability. Most likely, however, the trait of trusting that most other employees will also contribute to the common pool is very particular to *Danish* employees, so the flexicurity model may be hard to transfer elsewhere.

Generally, the evolution of Denmark's social and political systems has been smooth and steady, with early state formation and considerable political stability, compared with other countries. Actual sources documenting this are scarce, but some of the knowledge we do have indicates this reasoning is sound. We know, for instance, that in the Viking Age (early medieval times), peasants demanded to be protected from rival gangs. These roving Viking thugs would pillage randomly and at will, so the peasants were reluctant to invest. Why should they sow if they didn't know whether they would be able to reap?

This and other factors led to the early formation of state-like structures. The Norse chieftains with the best men and weaponry were powerful enough, and brutal enough, to set up a monopoly on violence. Surprisingly, a peaceful, well-ordered societal structure with clearly defined property rights evolved, enforced by the erstwhile roving thugs, who had more to gain by settling down and taxing the peasants. The result: Among Norsemen, the powerful lords would protect the peasants, who found it viable to increase production, since stealing other people's property had been made 'illegal'.

Higher production made the rulers *and* the populace richer, paving the way for investments in infrastructure, more trade and better security. One good example is the physical protection built around the early medieval town of Hedeby, which lies south of today's Danish–German border. Hedeby was one of the largest Viking Age trading hubs in Northern Europe, and security in the surrounding borderlands was upgraded through repeated expansions of Dannevirke, a system of ancient earthwork fortifications stretching some 30 kilometres.

The Vikings who landed on foreign shores over a thousand years ago did more than rape and plunder. They may have been ruthless pirates, but they also ended up as state-builders who effectively monopolised violence in the countries they settled. Posterity has probably underestimated their significance in this context – though indeed their benign influence was hardly intentional, but rather a coincidence of their modus operandi. Be that as it may, part of the widespread legacy of the Norsemen lay in defining and enforcing property rights. This promoted wealth and predictability, which in turn caused trust to accumulate over time.

The expression 'to keep one's word' is actually rooted in the ancient Norse languages. Listening to Icelandic (a cousin of modern Danish, Norwegian and Swedish) is the closest we can get to hearing what Vikings sounded like. In Icelandic, the wording in the norm of trust is: *orð skulu standa*, or 'words shall stand' unchanged in the future. The oldest written source that documents the phrase (as a rule of conduct) is the Icelandic code of the *Jónsbók* from 1281: *Svo skal hvert orð vera sem mælt er* – 'So shall every word be, as it is spoken'.

Trust is a hot research topic, and many international scholars have zoomed in on trustful countries such as Denmark to study its origins. However, it is also important to understand how social trust can disappear. We know that if too many people cheat, the system breaks down: If most people cheat, the population no longer has anything to gain from trusting each other.

As noted earlier, Denmark and Poland are illustrative examples. In the latter 1800s, the co-operative movement was growing and working equally well in both countries. Later, after Poland was knocked back first by the Russians, then by World War II, then by the Russians again, trust there evaporated. That's what happens when your neighbour is suddenly picked up by men in dark coats, never to return. Today, social trust in Poland is four times lower than in the peaceful fairy-tale country of Denmark.

TRUST
OR
CONTROL?

At first glance, control may seem alluring: Get a firm grip on the economy, increase control and step up assessments of public institutions. But beware: This strategy may easily backfire. The more control citizens are subjected to, the more superfluous they will find their collective trust reserve.

Trust and control are not necessarily opposites, but a well-balanced mix is always advisable. All else being equal, increased surveillance of citizens to prevent terrorism does create more security and social trust than if nothing were done. The same goes for automatic traffic monitoring to reveal speeding. Social media like Facebook are also a sort of surveillance, albeit voluntary and non-hierarchical, and in such tech-based social activities people communicate about almost everything, often sharing very personal information with audiences far beyond their circle of close friends.

But imagine that a government began to excessively check, say, local authorities, obliging them, in turn, to keep municipal institutions and employees on a tight leash. The politicians would be gambling with one of their country's most valuable resources. Denmark, where control is on the rise, could be a case in point. Trust is useless if everything is monitored and people are treated as if they can't be trusted. Put simply: 100% control means 0% trust. Control may force a few slackers to work a bit more, but if the many hard-working people are met with distrust, they may work less.

Unnecessary control in a country like Denmark involves an imminent risk of depleting trust. More control and documentation, which may seem like quality assurance of public-sector or political work, may turn out to be a costly exercise. Not just because resources are spent on superfluous control measures, but also because the bedrock on which Denmark's success was built will erode. Gradually, little leaks will drain the pool of trust that keeps the raft afloat. Conversely, if trust is used and stimulated the pool will be replenished, improving the bottom line for public organisations and private corporations, and promoting economic growth.

Danes, today the world's most trusting people, could quickly slip down the trust ladder if we allow the control society to take over. Schools, hospitals, nursing homes, municipal unemployment projects and scores of other public institutions and programmes find themselves in a transitional phase, as society moves from trust to control. Politicians want proof that those receiving large sums of the Danish taxpayers' money really are delivering the goods. Some use the term 'control', which has negative connotations, while others use the term 'quality assurance', which sounds positive. Terminology aside, municipal home-care staff must now use a hand-held device to log the time spent with each elderly citizen, and cleaning staff must log time and initials on a wall chart every time they've cleaned a restroom.

These are examples of a society that checks and documents to make sure nobody cheats or is cheated, and Denmark is moving in this direction today. It seems absurd to intensify control of the world's most trusting population. Control should be limited to areas where it is called for: moonlighting, social fraud, traffic violations, and other areas where financial or other crime can easily occur – the sort of areas where Danes tend to be trustful in that naive, Nordic sort of way. Apart from this, surveillance and control will often prove more costly in a high-trust society than simply trusting people.

In Denmark's case, if we really end up replacing the legend of King Frode Fredegod's golden ring, left by the roadside for later retrieval, with fireproof safes for our valuables, and if we end up replacing the relaxed horseback rides of King Christian X through the streets of Copenhagen with a sovereign who is forced to take cover behind bodyguards and anti-terror legislation, it will be very costly for our society.

It is debatable whether social trends can make Danish trust wither and die, yet even in the most stable of societies anxiety can grow, and trust can be undermined by factors such as police misconduct, gang violence, social fraud, political deceit, terrorist threats and generalised distrust among social or ethnic groups. An important message for Danes, and others, to take away from this discussion is: We must *not* take high social trust for granted. Trust can erode or evaporate in no time – as in Poland under Communist rule.

There are also other, less visible and dramatic threats than a Communist takeover. Escalating control of citizens and public employees may undermine trust, even if the original objective was the opposite: to prevent fraud and reassure the population that they can trust the public systems to work. Danish workplaces traditionally encourage self-organisation, and employers largely trust people to do their jobs. Trust, praise and recognition may stimulate people to make an extra effort. This sort of 'invisible' economy is based on reciprocity, and on the unspoken rules of gift-giving: I scratch your back, then hope you will scratch mine.

People exchange gifts based on trust, throwing an item or service into a network without any guarantee of reciprocation. In such exchanges gifts must be recognisable as gifts, and so they must be suitably proportioned: not so small that they fail to stimulate commitments or reciprocal gifts, and not so large that they embarrass recipients who can't reciprocate. When a gift is given, the recipient incurs a 'social debt', implying an expectation of future reciprocation, but with no calculation or demand as to the nature or timing of the gift. The recipient's conscience determines whether they wish to reciprocate or to freeride, in the latter case enjoying the value of the gift without contributing.

Trust is an important element in modern workplaces, public and private, where teamwork and knowledge-sharing are essential preconditions for innovation. Danes generally believe that delegating tasks based on trust rather than on control will motivate employees to devise novel solutions and think out of the box – vital processes in today's information societies.

A key ingredient in the recipe for a good workplace is: trust, trust, and more trust, with management not interfering in every little detail. Imagine a manager who delegates responsibility and shows trust in her subordinates. It's like she is giving them a gift, and they feel inclined to reciprocate and make an extra effort. Inversely, a manager who checks on her staff constantly is showing she doesn't trust them, and as a result they will behave accordingly.

Studies show that productivity and quality levels increase when a company shows trust in its employees. The work environment improves, and staff illness declines. Employees are more contented when they feel trusted, and their performance is higher, too. All these findings indicate it is wise for companies to take employee views on board when developing new strategies. Consider the example of home-care assistants. If they feel their municipal employer doesn't trust them, they won't feel like making an extra effort. Instead, they may actually feel inclined to start cutting corners. This is bad for productivity, and in an emerging Big Brother scenario like this, social trust is lost.

So why is the control approach slowly gaining ground? One main reason in Denmark is that typically, when a flaw in the system is publicised and pursued by the media, politicians advocate more control, promising that augmented control will prevent similar episodes. Laws that increase control based on unfortunate, one-off episodes is an easy solution, but it is also short-sighted and may lead towards a slippery slope. A control society is expensive, and controllers, too, must be monitored. Some degree of control is unavoidable, but excessive control is a waste of resources – and it makes going to work a lot less enjoyable.

Russia initially seemed to have learned from the past as it began moving away from cumbersome, control-based systems after 1991. The goal was to create a political system that citizens would view as appealing rather than objectionable. Trust between Russia's civil society and the state apparatus was on the rise, as new foreign investors commended the work ethic and initiative of Russian employees while providing them with decent working conditions. These lessons were also beginning to influence companies owned and operated by Russians. However, the renewed centralization of power and the unprovoked invasion of Ukraine underscore that Russia still has a long way to go.

It is fair to conclude that if we want to utilise trust, control ought to be minimised – and the fewer resources we expend to make things work, the more resources we can use to improve competition, advance research and nurture innovation. The whole point is to optimise the mix of trust and control while not exaggerating either, bearing in mind that the more trust there is in a population, the less need there is to monitor it. This is an advantage that Denmark, most trusting of nations, ought to exploit to its fullest.

When people begin to doubt that others will pitch in, or when formal institutions start to pursue their own goals rather than society's best interests, trust suffers. Even Denmark may see the emergence of a vicious circle of increasing tax evasion, lower tax revenues, and less money for public investments and services. This would further weaken the population's trust in the system, leading to more tax evasion and so on, in a downward spiral. Picture a swirling vortex, inexorably sucking the Danish welfare raft towards the bottom as the great pool of trust empties. Without tax revenues, the welfare state will simply cease to exist. In other words, the level of social trust must be sustained in order to preserve the welfare state and maintain the integrity of the labour-market flexicurity models and other central beams in the welfare raft.

The great challenge for Denmark's future in this globalised world will be to sustain and strengthen the country's world record in trust. The Danish gold will be all too easily squandered if the norms supporting high trust and low corruption disintegrate.

If we Danes want our welfare state to survive in the long term, it is crucial that the country's government, cultural institutions, families and schools uphold essential behavioural norms and rules. These include keeping our word, and being honest, fair and equal before the law. It is just as crucial that all able-bodied citizens pitch in, and that we commend those who contribute and keep their word while chastising those who don't. This will help Denmark maintain the solid foundation of trust on which our welfare state rests.

Looking forward, researchers have to study how trust is generated and destroyed. Our knowledge of trust creation remains especially limited, and in a global perspective, trust may turn out to be a crucial competitive parameter.

I already mentioned the phrase famously attributed to Lenin: that trust is good, but control is better. Let me rephrase that: "Control is good, but trust is cheaper." Trust pays off, pure and simple, so wherever trust can replace control, it should be used. Trust is just a cheaper way to run a society, so in the future, companies and public organisations alike should play the trust card when dealing with their employees, for everyone's sake. And besides saving money, trust is linked to *hygge*, another important part of the Danish mentality. If you're not convinced yet, dear reader, take a trip to Durban by way of Læsø and you will realise that trust is, indeed, Denmark's gold.

It's late in the evening and the sun is setting. The Durban conference is several years behind me, and I am camping on a small Danish island with part of my clan:

Gunnar and our wives and children. A bumblebee flies by. We sit around our folding table exchanging smiles, each holding a knife in one hand and a fork in the other, and feeling deeply thankful. When the kids are asleep, I will find a nice, cosy spot and spend some time on my new manuscript. It's all about trust.